This book belongs to

_____

This edition published by Parragon Books Ltd in 2017

Parragon Books Ltd
Chartist House
15–17 Trim Street
Bath BA1 1HA, UK
www.parragon.com

Illustrated by: Giuditta Gaviraghi
Reading consultant: Geraldine Taylor

ISBN 978-1-4748-6306-3

Printed in China

FIRST READERS

Jack and the Beanstalk

Parragon

Bath · New York · Cologne · Melbourne · Delhi
Hong Kong · Shenzhen · Singapore

Five steps for enjoyable reading

Traditional stories and fairy tales are a great way to begin reading practice. The stories and characters are familiar and lively. Follow the steps below to help your child become a confident and independent reader.

Step 1
Read the story aloud to your child. Run your finger under the words as you read.

Step 2
Look at the pictures and talk about what is happening.

One day, Jack's mum said, "We have no money and nothing to eat. Take our cow to market and sell her, so that we can buy some food."

Jack took the cow to market. He swapped the cow for some magic beans.

8

Step 3

Read the simple text on the right-hand page together. When reading, some words come up again and again, such as **the**, **to** or **and**. Your child will quickly learn to recognize these high-frequency words by sight.

Jack ran all the way home with his bag of beans.

9

Step 4

When your child is ready, encourage them to read the simple lines on their own.

Step 5

Help your child to complete the puzzles at the back of the book.

One day, Jack's mum said, "We have no money and nothing to eat. Take our cow to market and sell her, so that we can buy some food."

Jack took the cow to market. He swapped her for some magic beans.

Jack ran all the way home with his bag of beans.

When Jack's mum saw the beans, she was cross.

"Silly boy!" shouted Jack's mum. "Now we have no cow, no money and nothing to eat!"

She threw the beans into the garden and sent Jack to bed.

Jack went off to bed. He was sad
about the beans.

The next morning, Jack looked out of his window. There was a giant beanstalk in the garden!

Jack was hungry. He climbed the beanstalk to look for some beans to eat.

He climbed up and up, into the clouds.

Jack went all the
way to the top of the
giant beanstalk.

At the top of the beanstalk, Jack found a giant castle. He knocked at the door. The cook opened the door.

"Please may I have something to eat?" asked Jack.

The cook gave him some food. Then they heard footsteps.

"You must hide!" she cried. "The giant who lives here likes to eat little boys for his supper!"

Boom, boom, boom!
Jack hid in a cupboard.

The bad, greedy giant stomped into the kitchen.

"Fee-fi-fo-fum, I smell the blood of a little boy!" the giant shouted.

"Don't be silly," said the cook. "You can smell these sausages."

Jack was scared.
Would the giant
eat him?

The greedy giant ate the sausages.

"Bring me my gold!" roared
the giant.

The cook got his gold and the
greedy giant counted it.

Soon, the giant fell asleep. Jack
popped out of the cupboard and
grabbed a bag of gold!

Jack quickly climbed back down the beanstalk with the bag of gold.

Jack's mum bought some food. But, soon, all the gold was gone and they were hungry again.

Jack climbed up the beanstalk again. He hid in the castle.

Soon, the greedy giant came into the kitchen.

"Fee-fi-fo-fum, I smell the blood of a little boy!" he shouted.

"Don't be silly," said the cook. "You can smell meat."

The giant ate the meat.

21

"Bring me my hen!" roared the greedy giant. The cook fetched a fat, white hen. The hen laid a big, golden egg!

As soon as the giant fell asleep, Jack popped out and grabbed the hen.

Jack climbed down the
beanstalk with the fat,
white hen.

The next day, Jack climbed the beanstalk again. He hid in the castle and waited for the giant to come.

"Bring me my harp!" roared the giant.

The cook got a golden harp. It played to the giant. He fell asleep.

Jack popped out and grabbed the harp – but the giant woke up!

"Fee-fi-fo-fum!" he cried.
"Stop! Come back, boy!"

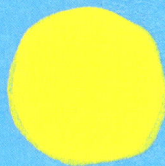

Jack climbed down the beanstalk as fast as he could go. The giant chased after him.

Jack got to the bottom and grabbed an axe. He chopped down the beanstalk.

Crash! The giant fell to the ground.

And that was the end of the
bad, greedy giant.

Puzzle time!

Which two words rhyme?

top   can   red   mum   bed

Which word does not match the picture?

bean
magic
cow

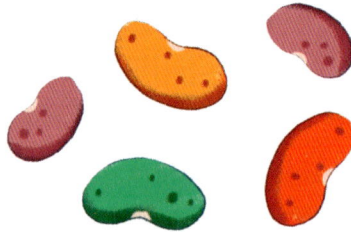

Which word matches the picture?

gold
hold
told

Who hid in the castle?

Jack

giant

mum

Which sentence is right?

"Fee-fi-fo-fum!" said the giant.

"Fo-fum-fee-fi!" said the giant.